THE 9 SIGNS OF

EFFECTIVE LEADERSHIP

*A **CONCISE** handbook of what effective leaders know*
*. . . and aspiring leaders **NEED** to know*

DR. TONY BOLDEN

© Copyright 2012, 2022 – Tony Bolden Enterprises LLC

For more information about Tony Bolden Enterprises LLC Please Contact:

Email: Tony@TonyBoldenSpeaks.com

Web: www.TonyBoldenSpeaks.com

I dedicate this book to every effective leader.
You have proven that you are qualified to lead others to
success.

I also dedicate this book to every aspiring leader.
You have answered the call to leadership, and
understand that learning and growing will only make you
more effective!

What Is A *"Leader"*? 6

Chapter 1: Flexibility.. 11

Chapter 2: Low Aversion to Risk... 16

Chapter 3: Knowledgeable 20

Chapter 4: Visionary 30

Chapter 5: Change Resilient 34

Chapter 6: Strategic.. 38

Chapter 7: Communicator 45

Chapter 8: Motivator... 49

Chapter 9: Learner... 53

Final Thoughts: Where do you go from here?..................... 57

About the Author 59

The 9 Signs of Effective Leadership Quiz 60

Referenced Resources 63

The 9 Signs "Take Action!" Workbook.................................. 65

What Is A *"Leader"*?

What exactly is a leader? Isn't that the question of the ages? We've all heard the term throughout our lives, but as a whole we can't quite seem to grasp the true meaning of the word "leader." If asked, most of us would say that a leader is *"someone in charge."* In his 1997 book *An Integrative Theory of Leadership,* Martin Chemers asserted that leadership is *"a process of social influence in which one person is able to enlist the aid and support of others in the accomplishment of a common task."* Additionally, Ralph Stogdill conducted an exhaustive review of the study of leadership and concluded that *"there are almost as many definitions of leadership as there are persons who have*

attempted to define the concept." ("Leadership: A Survey of Literature", 1974).

In his 2007 article *The Challenges of Leadership in the Modern World*, Warren Bennis noted the lack of a single definition of leadership, affirming it as a nebulous area of study. Much has been written about leadership over the centuries – from contextual concepts to styles to theories – but the essence of the word leader can be found in its definition. Webster's New Collegiate Dictionary defines a leader as *"someone who leads: a person who has commanding authority or influence".* Essentially, you don't have to be the person in charge to be a leader...you just has to have *commanding authority or influence.*

At this point, it is also important to underscore the differences between the terms **leader** and **effective leader**. A **leader** is a leader by virtue of title. He or she may have been elected or appointed, but they have assumed a title. Some leaders have no discernible vision (or any extensive knowledge of the organization and their surroundings) but they have a "cool" title listed on their business cards. Many of us are either involved in or are aware of organizations where the president of the organization is not the leader. Sure, they have the title, but they have no authority. The Director of Marketing or the Finance Chairman has more influence than the entitled *"leader"* does.

Conversely, an **effective leader** is someone who uses his or her talents and abilities to enhance their organizations. They don't seek fame or attention, they simply seek to inspire those around them to be the very best that they can be. Every effective leader knows that in order for the organization to enjoy sustained success, those who work within the organization have to feel as though they are contributors to the overall vision. They must be viewed as "co-heirs" to the organization's success. Most leaders want to be *effective* leaders, but they haven't had many real life examples. Although we see the successful leaders of business, politics, and civic organizations in the press, many people don't have access to these leaders on a regular basis.

What do effective leaders know that separate them from the rest? How do they meet and exceed expectations and guide their organizations to greatness? One of the most productive ways to achieve success is to emulate the traits of those who are successful. I have been fortunate to enjoy a successful sales career that surpasses 20 years. In that time, I've worked with some of the most successful organizations in the world, and with some of the most innovative and successful leaders of industry. In that time, I've observed nine core traits that effective leaders share:

1. Flexibility

2. Low Aversion to Risk

3. Knowledgeable

4. Visionary

5. Change Resilient

6. Strategic

7. Communicator

8. Motivator

9. Learner

Are there more than nine core traits of effective leadership? Certainly. In fact, you might be able to identify *9,000* traits of effective leaders. I believe, however, that if you don't possess at least the nine listed above your tenure will be difficult at best – and disastrous at worst. Is there any one trait that is more important than the others? I don't think so. Although you may be a better communicator than a motivator, you still must be able to employ both. I don't profess to be **the** expert in leadership (there are already enough "experts" in this area of study). I'm simply a man who has had the pleasure of leading, and of associating with effective leaders. This concise book shouldn't be your bible on leadership. It's simply a testament of what I've learned and observed.

Chapter 1: Flexibility

Flexible leaders are able to adapt to dynamic environments. Henry David Thoreau once said *"man is an animal who more than any other can adapt himself to all climates and circumstances."* Every leader knows that in order to enjoy any measure of success, you have to be able to adapt to your environment. Most of us who have been in positions of leadership have inherited organizations that were not necessarily well- oiled machines. Maybe there were ineffective policies in place, or people within the organization that needed to be inspired to produce. Whatever the case, we rarely encounter opportunities for leadership that perfectly fit our preconceived notions.

Many of us have a vision that goes something like this:

You are appointed to the presidency of one of the largest corporations in the world. The stock is going through the roof, products are flying off the shelves, and all employees are happy and doing everything they can to ensure the company's success. You are a multi-billionaire with an expensive car, beautiful home and family. You are one of the most important people in business today.

Perhaps your goal isn't corporate leadership. Maybe your vision looks something like this:

You have been elected as the new president of one of the largest and oldest non-profit organizations in the world. The organization is receiving more donations than ever before. You work with a staff of volunteers that are selfless and extremely efficient. You have the ear of every politician and corporate "big-wig" in the country. You are well respected and your advice is sought around the world.

The previous scenarios are a bit abstract and lofty, but let's be honest: no one wants to inherit something that needs to be fixed. In reality, you were appointed, elected, or promoted to your leadership position because you are supposed to be the person who is capable of guiding the organization through its challenges. In his contribution to the book *The Organization of the Future*, Doug Miller noted that in the future, organizations must be led by those who can assume chameleon-like tendencies. These leaders must possess foundational flexibility and commit to moving, adapting, and changing as required by their environments.

As an effective leader, you almost have to think of yourself as a soldier: you must be flexible enough to adapt to any environment you find yourself in. I started my sales career more than 20 years ago as a telemarketer. I assumed the job would be "sales, primarily phone based", in actuality I found myself on the phone for 10 hours a day. I didn't inherit a profitable territory. In fact, I was giving a 3 foot high stack of dead leads and encouraged to make the best of them.

The job was far from glamorous, but I was determined to succeed nonetheless. I had nothing to lose, and everything to gain. I was a natural talker, so I adapted to the sales environment with ease and speed. I learned how to overcome objections and persuade my prospects to buy our product. Most importantly, I learned how to take what I was given and make the best of it. I eventually became the top inside salesman within the organization, and was promoted to the position of territory manager. Since I had proven I was capable of reviving dead leads, I assumed that I would be inheriting a thriving territory. Much to my surprise, I was again given a territory that needed substantial resuscitation.

I worked hard and turned the territory into a profit center in the organization, increasing territory revenue by 25% each year for three consecutive years. Am I a sales wizard? Hardly. I simply adapt to my environment and determine the best way to achieve my goals. Remember; effective leaders could be equated with battle-tested soldiers: they never lose focus of their goals – they identify different ways to accomplish the mission.

Chapter 2: Low Aversion to Risk

Effective leaders who have a low aversion to risk are able to manage appropriate risks and use them to the organization's advantage. We've all heard the expression *"you have to crack a few eggs to make an omelet"*, but do we truly understand what that means? We live in an era where people desire *more* but want to sacrifice *less* to get it. We don't like to venture beyond our comfort zones. We would rather club the lion across the head as he walks by, rather than going into the jungle and drag him out kicking and screaming.

I had the pleasure of working with consultant and author Bill Treasurer. Bill is a formidable facilitator, business coach, and top-notch consultant. He is also a former member of the U.S.

High Diving team, and he even acted as a "fire diver" – high-diving while ablaze. Bill authored a book titled *Right Risk* where he advocated fearlessly engaging in necessary risk to achieve goals. He wrote that *"to live is risk...risk-taking is as essential to life as breathing. It is the oxygen of such things as innovation, entrepreneurialism, leadership..."*. Bill truly identified with Frederick Wilcox's summation that *"progress always involves risk; you can't steal second base and keep your foot on first."*

Years ago I was privileged to coach a little league baseball team. One of the toughest techniques to teach small children is base-stealing. For most 7 and 8 year olds, reaching 1st base is a monumental accomplishment. The last thing a kid wants is to look into the dugout and see you signaling for them to steal second base on the next hit. There is a look of sheer panic that rushes across their faces as they wince in your direction. They're happy where they are...for all they care, the game could end immediately, and they'd be ecstatic to have had the opportunity to get to first base. As the coach, however, I knew that the only way to win a game was to round the bases. It was my job to motivate these kids to get off of the bag, and run like their lives depended on it.

The kids on my baseball team learned the same lesson that effective leaders have learned: all progress involves risk taking. Sometimes it's measured, other times it's pure death defying, cliff jumping risk...but, it's risk nonetheless. In these perilous economic times, companies all across the world have closed their doors because they couldn't keep up with the demands of their marketplace. The landscape has become a treacherous, slippery slope of constantly changing ideas, trends, and economic potholes. You can't continue to use time-worn traditions and methodologies to woo customers in this new economy. You must be able to move outside of your comfort zone and take a risk; do things differently, venture into the unknown for a change.

That said, to be an effective leader you must be able to take and manage *appropriate* risks to advance your organization. We've heard the stories of leaders who have driven their organizations into the ground because they took risks that were far too great for the enterprise to absorb. Unwise financial decisions, questionable product releases, and neglectful labor practices are all examples of recklessly risky behavior. You shouldn't make a decision just because you're the boss. As an effective leader, it is absolutely imperative that you consider the consequences before you make a move. An effective leader's goal is to take and manage appropriate risks that are to the organizations advantage, not its detriment. Anyone can sit at the helm and make decisions on a whim, but an effective leader aspires to more than that: their goal is to use sound judgment to guide the enterprise toward success.

Chapter 3: Knowledgeable

Effective leaders must be knowledgeable about trends, practices, and policies affecting their industries and organizations. Benjamin Disraeli noted *"The more extensive a man's knowledge of what has been done, the greater will be his power of knowing what to do."* In their book *Knowledge Management: Challenges, Solutions, and Technologies*, authors Irma Becerra-Fernandez, Avelino Gonzalez, and Rajiv Sabherwal offer a more simplistic view of knowledge – considering it to be at the apex in a hierarchy were information resides at the middle level, and data languishes at the lowest level. The authors noted that *"knowledge refers to information that enables action and decisions, or information with direction. Hence, knowledge is intrinsically similar to information and data, although it is the*

richest and deepest of the three, and is consequently also the most valuable."

Similarly, in their book *Knowledge Emergence: Social, technical, and evolutionary dimensions of knowledge creation,* Ikujiro Nonaka and Toshihiro Nishiguchi wrote:

Knowledge is context-specific and relational. Knowledge is dynamic, as it is dynamically created in social interactions. Knowledge is also humanistic, and it has both an active and a subjective nature. For the purposes of this study, we define knowledge as 'a dynamic human process of justifying personal belief toward the truth.

Knowledge differs from information. Information is non-humanistic because it exists without human interaction or attachment to a personal belief system. Knowledge, as suggested by Nonaka and Nishiguchi, is reliant upon humanistic involvement for its existence. Essentially, knowledge is information that facilitates action.

According to Becerra-Fernandez, Gonzalez, and Sabherwal, knowledge discovery is *"the development of new tacit or explicit knowledge from data and information or from the synthesis of prior knowledge."* Knowledge discovery relies on explicit knowledge (where multiple sources of data/information are combined to create new knowledge) and tacit knowledge (where individuals create knowledge through joint activities as opposed to written instruction or directions). Becerra-Fernandez et al subsequently contended that knowledge capture is *"the process of retrieving either explicit or tacit knowledge that resides within people, artifacts, or organizational entities."*

At times, knowledge may reside within the mind, where the possessor lacks the ability to recognize and share it with others. Likewise, explicit knowledge may be available (such as a policy manual or standard operating procedures) but many may be unaware of its existence. Becerra – Fernandez et al asserted that the focus of knowledge capture is the importance of obtaining tacit knowledge from the mind and explicit knowledge from manuals so that the knowledge can be shared.

Explicit and tacit knowledge complement one another, and both are equally important for the acquisition of knowledge. Nonaka and Nishiguchi contended that knowledge conversion (the interaction between tacit and explicit knowledge) is a vital element in the knowledge creation (and subsequently, acquisition) process. Even though knowledge resides within individuals, things, and organizations, knowledge acquisition occurs when these varying elements interact with one another. According to Nonaka and Nishiguchi, the four modes of knowledge conversion (or acquisition) are:

1. Socialization (from tacit knowledge to tacit knowledge)

2. Externalization (from tacit knowledge to explicit knowledge)

3. Combination (from explicit knowledge to explicit knowledge)

4. Internalization (from explicit knowledge to tacit knowledge)

In socialization, tacit-to-tacit knowledge is acquired when possessors interact through joint activities and share same experiences (such as spending time with one another and living in the same environment), capitalizing on the core strength of socialization – physical proximity. An example of successful socialization throughout history is the concept of apprenticeships, where skilled persons transfer knowledge with eager learners by guiding and mentoring (over time).

In externalization, tacit-to-explicit knowledge is acquired through the expression of words (such as metaphors), concepts (hypothesis), and visual language (models, diagrams, and prototypes), thereby accommodating various modes of learning for everyone involved in the knowledge exchange. Generally, externalization benefits from two key factors: deductive and inductive analysis techniques aid in the expression of ideas, and deductive and inductive reasoning helps to translate information into readily understandable forms.

In combination, explicit-to-explicit knowledge is acquired when possessors exchange information through various media (such as email, meetings, and telephone conversations). Further, existing knowledge is "broken down" in order to aid in the creation of even newer knowledge. The combination process facilitates the further justification of knowledge in order to establish the basis for agreement, and to allow those seeking knowledge to initiate practical application. Combination relies on three specific processes.

A.   Explicit knowledge is gathered (either internally or externally from an organization) then combined.

B.   This new explicit knowledge is disseminated throughout the organization (via presentations or meetings).

C.   The new explicit knowledge is then processed within the organization for future utilization.

Modern technological networking functionality (such as instant messaging and social networking) further facilitates the use of combination.

In internalization, explicit-to-tacit knowledge is acquired by "doing" – essentially transferred throughout an organization through on-the-job application and "know how." Internalization relies on two dimensions:

A.   Explicit knowledge must be embraced and practiced. In doing so, the process of internalizing explicit knowledge brings life to concepts and strategies (as an example, formal on-boarding and training programs help contributors understand the organization and their own roles and responsibilities).

B.   Explicit knowledge may be embraced through experiential learning (role playing, scenario-based learning, and so on). These scenarios allow knowledge to be presented in "real world" illustrations, thus increasing the likelihood of adoption.

This detailed exploration of knowledge serves as a beacon to cast light on the importance of knowledge attainment and distribution in the tenure of an effective leader. The nature, purpose, and acquisition (or capturing) of knowledge has been concisely explored and discussed, but this exploration would be futile if effective leaders lacked plans of knowledge application. Becerra-Fernandez et al concluded *"...it can be argued that the most vital resource of today's enterprise is the collective knowledge residing in the minds of an organization's employees, customers, and vendors."* If this is true, then effective leaders must understand that knowledge is one of the lifelines of a successful organization. Organizational performance is greatly impacted when knowledge is used to make decisions and perform specific tasks. Further, organizational leaders run the risk of stifling future knowledge discovery and sharing if a perceived (or realized) bottleneck effect exists. Knowledge application is simply praxis – putting knowledge into practice.

As a leader, you can't fully understand the direction in which the organization should be moving towards if you have no knowledge of where it's been. First, you must have a working knowledge of past policies, practices, and trends that have affected the organization. Has there been a clear channel of communication within the organization? Has the organization always operated within its budget or have there been any overruns? Have there been any serious personnel issues? Overall, is the organization operating above or below expectations? Secondly, you must have a working knowledge of policies, practices, and trend that are affecting your industry. Is the organization complying with applicable laws? Are operations comparative to similar organizations with the industry? What trends are expected to impact the industry in the future? You can't just operate in a vacuum. You have to know what you're working with.

Early in my sales career, I learned the importance of knowledge gathering and application – and I learned my lesson the hard way. I received a call from a prospect that was very eager to place a large order for my product. I got the basic information I needed to place the order, but I didn't ask the important questions that would establish a productive relationship for the future. A few weeks later, I received a call from my new customer. I learned that the person who placed the order wasn't authorized to do so. Additionally, the product I sold was not what the customer needed. I would have known that if I asked questions. I had no knowledge of the trends that affected my customer, or even why they felt they needed that particular product. I was only interested in placing the order – and the immediate gratification. Because of my lack of knowledge, I sold them the wrong product, and had to return their money. Knowledge is power, and the more knowledge you have, the better prepared you are to lead your organization effectively.

Chapter 4: Visionary

Effective leaders are visionaries because they create and communicate an inspired sense of purpose. These leaders lead with a vision of the future, and not just the reality of today. Webster defines "visionary" as *"tending to envision things in perfect but unrealistic form; idealistic."* While I agree with the majority of the definition, I take exception to the term "unrealistic." I fervently believe that to be an effective leader, you must lead with a vision of the future – your desired state – and not be encumbered or deterred by the circumstances you find in your current state. Think of the leaders you have met in your life who couldn't think or see beyond their current state. They were trapped in the systematic way of doing things because they couldn't see the bigger picture. I contend that many ineffective leaders find themselves consumed with the challenges that they see every day instead of focusing on the opportunities that lie beyond those challenges.

In their book *Virtuoso Teams: Lessons From Teams That Changed Their Worlds*, Andy Boynton and Bill Fisher wrote that strong leaders *"...powerfully drive the team, its vision, culture, and the results"*, further noting that these leaders *"...drive a powerful, very ambitious vision into the fabric of their team."* Dr. Sooksan Kantabutra (international leadership researcher and lecturer) noted that vision is an important element in successful sustainability strategies and organizational performance. Specifically, Dr. Kantabutra asserted that vision (and by extension, corporate vision as cast by an effective leader) should be simple with broad meaning so that stakeholders (internal and external) can be inspired and challenged to contribute.

Some leaders believe that having a vision qualifies them for sainthood, and their vision immediately propels them into the stratosphere of success. Truth be told, vision is simply the identification, understanding, and declaration of a desired future state. For example, I have a vision of living a completely healthy life, so accordingly my vision statement may read: "My vision is to be happy and in good health." That declaration alone doesn't create the inertia necessary to ensure my success. Noted business paradigm consultant Joel Barker once said *"vision without action is merely a dream; action without vision just passes the time: vision with action can change the world."*

Vision without execution is a dream, so effective leaders must cast their vision while simultaneously portraying the practicality (and achievability) of their goals to their followers. Visionary leaders look out across their horizons and see the direction they want to move toward, the challenges and opportunities for advancement that lie ahead, and a representation of what they hope to achieve. These same leaders don't look ahead without taking stock in their current circumstances. Rather, these leaders are able to navigate through and beyond the present because they've seen a glimpse of what lies ahead...and that motivates and propels them forward.

Chapter 5: Change Resilient

Effective leaders must be able to cope with and embrace change, and also use it to their advantage. Change is one of the most uncomfortable realities in business – and in life. Nothing remains the same...at least nothing that expects to grow. Organizations must evolve and change to respond to the constant ebb and flow of their constituents. Moreover, leaders and team members within those organizations should also be prepared to adjust. In his 2004 article "Who Me, Change?" Peter de Jager wrote that change is simply *"something that happens when something moves from one situation to another."*

Early in my speaking career, I frequently discussed the fear of change. It's difficult to embrace change because of the uncertainty involved...the lack of sure-fire guarantees. Someone once told me *"if you want a guarantee, buy a major appliance and keep the receipt."* Many of us go through life trying to avoid change. We don't want to move too far from our comfort zones, so we sacrifice growth for the sake of stability – a guarantee. Whenever I spoke of change during speaking engagements, I always shared a personal story about how I made a life-changing decision to move from Chicago to Atlanta.

In the early 1990's, I was offered a raise and a relocation package from my then-employer. I was young, childless, and single, so a relocation decision should have been quick and easy to make. The fact that I struggled with my decision (for a long time) was an example of me being deeply entrenched in my comfort zone. At the time, I thought that I was pretty change resilient, but this episode clearly illustrated that I had a lot more growing to do. I was eventually able to use that change event to my own advantage. Eighteen years later, I have a lovely family and reside in the suburbs of Atlanta, Georgia. In hindsight, I can't imagine what my life would be like had I stayed in Chicago, but I had to be confronted with change before I ever thought about venturing out of my comfort zone.

In his book *The Path of Least Resistance*, Robert Fritz distinguished between *effective* people and *ineffective* people. Fritz noted that ineffective people have a tendency to operate in a reactive-responsive mode of behavior much of the time. Instead of consciously and deliberately choosing their courses of action, they react to what is going on around them (and respond negatively according to their emotions). Ineffective people are constantly riding an emotional roller coaster. In this mode of behavior, the best that they can hope for is to get back to middle ground (or "even"), where they were before they became upset. Conversely, the *effective* person focuses on the post-change future. Whenever an unexpected change or setback occurs, the effective person immediately focuses his or her mind on where they want to be at a future time.

When change events occur, effective leaders don't worry about what happened. Rather, these leaders shift their focus towards what they need to do next. If you spend your time reacting to every situation that occurs during your leadership tenure, you'll never have time to focus on the future. Remember, as an effective leader you are responsible for the direction of your organization. If your vision is clouded or interrupted by the constant changes that occur, you can't clearly see what lies ahead.

Chapter 6: Strategic

Effective leaders must be strategic – they must be able to see ahead clearly and anticipate consequences and trends accurately. I consider this competency of effective leadership to be my strongest trait. I have an affinity for strategic planning. In fact, my wife thinks that I plan too much (as a result, my weakest competency is being change resilient). I am of the belief if you fail to plan, then you're certainly planning to fail. I simply can't identify with people who roll out of bed on a work day and think to themselves *"Hmm, what am I going to do today?"*

As a career sales professional, I was taught long ago that you should plan at least two weeks ahead in order to have enough activities to create revenue. I learned early in my career that it was considered a mortal sin to not have your calendar filled with appointments for the next few weeks. Effective leaders are strategic when charting the course for their organizations. They aren't *obsessed* with their plans; they simply understand how important it is to have plans. This could be a tricky high wire act to navigate: how can you be an effective leader with a low aversion to risk and be change resilient while simultaneously being grounded enough to be a strategic planner and thinker?

Clearly, you must have balance. Sometimes you must act quickly and make decisions based on your knowledge and instinct, but you shouldn't always be in "reactive" mode (remember what Robert Fritz said about effective and ineffective people). In his seminal book *Pathways to Performance*, Jim Clemmer wrote that strategy is *"an interactive process. It might be separated from daily management, but can't it be separated from leadership. It is leadership."* As an effective leader, you can't expect those in your organization to successfully implement and execute a strategic plan if you haven't done so yourself. This *"do as I say"* attitude is akin to telling your children to eat their vegetables if they want to be strong and healthy...as you avoid vegetables at all costs.

Effective leaders must be adept at establishing and implementing strategic plans. I had the pleasure of working with Michael Wilkinson for several years. Wilkinson is the Managing Director of Leadership Strategies in Atlanta, GA – and a world-renown facilitator. He asserted that the strategic planning process is critical to organizational health since it establishes corporate direction, and defines the detailed results and tactics that will aid in achieving the desired direction. Wilkinson created the drivers model (below) that illustrates the strategic planning process – from situational assessment to implementation. The model takes what I consider a comprehensive organizational process and collapses it into digestible steps that should be easily understood.

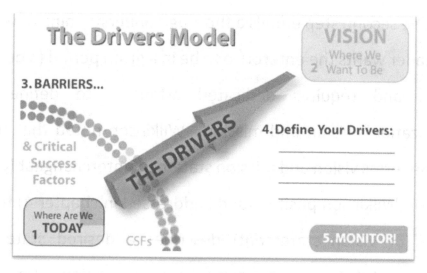

Figure - The Drivers Model - Leadership Strategies, Inc. image credit

The Drivers Model is a process methodology employed to help organizations identify and solve business problems, but it's also an illustration of how effective leadership methodically strategize an approach to problem solving and goal attainment. The first step of the methodology is an assessment of the organizations current state, where leaders should ask *"where are we today?"* With no fundamental understanding of what currently works (or does not), the leader could begin a quest for goal attainment without understanding his or her existing shortfalls.

The second step entails a thorough understanding of where the leader wants the enterprise to be in a given period (a desired state), and requires dedicated attention to define the organization's vision and mission. Wilkinson noted that some use the terms vision and mission statement interchangeably, but in error. Wilkinson posited (and I addressed in chapter 4) that a vision (or vision statement) describes a desired state (for example, 100% debt-freedom), but a mission statement describes how the vision will be achieved (for example, using cash instead of credit, eliminating impulse purchases, and more). This step also includes defining the organization's goals (broad and long-term) and objectives (short-term and quantifiable).

The third step includes examination of critical success factors and barriers to successful goal attainment. Critical success factors are key conditions and elements necessary to aid in organizational achievement (for example, budget approval, talent assessment, and more). Barriers are clear roadblocks that could impede successful implementation of the new system design (for example, entrenched organizational culture, talent gaps, and more). The fourth step in this process is identification of drivers – the strategies developed to move the organization from current to future state. Some consider strategies to be a clear roadmap that systematically illustrates a step-by-step process to drive organizational momentum toward the desired state. These strategies should be prioritized to ensure that less important strategies do not disrupt momentum, and that high-priority strategies receive due attention.

The fifth and final step in the process is monitoring progress. Wilkinson noted that plans are simply calls to action, but the substantive work is the implementation of those plans and the continual measurement and refinement to ensure those plans maintain momentum and achieve results. Once the strategic plan is designed and implemented, the effective leader must articulate this plan clearly throughout the organization. You must let every subordinate know what's expected, and give them realistic goals to achieve. You should also be prepared to reward achievement and motivate those who are struggling.

Remember: an effective leader is tasked with inspiring everyone in the organization to be the best that they can be, and to contribute to the overall success of an organization. Plan your work, and WORK YOUR PLAN!

Chapter 7: Communicator

An effective leader is a communicator who relates well to diverse stakeholders inside and outside the organization. These leaders are able to influence and stimulate others, and build constructive relationships. It's useless to be a creative, innovative leader if you can't successfully communicate your vision to those around you. As the leader, it's your job to see the vision and be able to articulate it to others. You can't envision and execute all by yourself. You need others to essentially be your arms and legs within the organization.

One of the hallmarks of sound leadership is the ability to communicate effectively. I believe that leaders have an even greater responsibility to ensure that those whom we communicate with are able to process the information given. Effective leaders are expected to establish direct paths of communication so that subordinates receive instruction that is unmistakably clear. Similarly, leaders must also receive unfettered feedback from subordinates to help them make appropriate adjustments. In his book *Team Players and Teamwork: New Strategies for Developing Successful Collaboration*, Glenn Parker noted that a leader who is also an effective communicator possess unique traits for leading a team. Parker wrote that the communicative leader *"...believes strongly that people who are closest to the problem should be deeply involved in the development of the solution."*

At its core, communication entails the sending and receiving of information (both verbally and non-verbally). Ideally, senders and receivers are equally responsible for ensuring that clear communication takes place. Senders have an obligation to speak clearly (both in enunciation and intent), succinctly, and matter-of-factly to ensure that their words are easily understood by receivers.

Receivers have an obligation to engage in active listening, which involves sensing (receiving all cues emitted verbally and nonverbally), processing (mentally processing the material that has been received by understanding, interpreting, evaluating, and remembering it), and responding (assuring that listening has occurred and encouraging further communication through verbal and nonverbal cues). This communication model works in ideal circumstances. The stark reality, however, is that the sender must do everything *(within reason)* to ensure that he or she communicates clearly and are easily understood – especially when the sender is a leader.

Of course, communication must be more than just a verbal exercise. Dr. David Thomas of Harvard Business School once said *"what you say is only the beginning...your behavior, your actions, and your decisions are also ways of communicating, and leaders have to learn how to create a consistent message through all of these."* Effective leaders encourage their followers by modeling the behavior they want to see in their followers. As an effective leader, you can communicate a message to those around you not only by opening your mouth, but by also offering yourself as a living example of what commitment to success looks like.

Chapter 8: Motivator

Effective leaders are able to inspire, motivate, and persuade others. Media mogul Rupert Murdoch once said *"In motivating people, you've got to engage their minds and their hearts. I motivate people, I hope, by example -- and perhaps by excitement, by having productive ideas to make others feel involved."* You have to inspire those around you to reach for greatness if you want your organization to enjoy sustained success. Your followers should be as excited about the future as you are...no one wants to work for or with someone who doesn't engage their minds. Everyone wants to feel like they belong to *something*. We all want to feel excited about our contribution to the success of the organization. An effective leader's role is to engage the hearts and minds of those who toil with them day in and day out.

One of the best ways to get something done is to motivate those around you to *help* you do it. Your followers are more inclined to contribute within the organization when you seek *their* help in doing what needs to be done. That said, an effective leader doesn't make the mistake of casting him or herself as Cheerleader-in-Chief. Motivation cannot be endowed upon someone through *"rah rah – you can do it!"* sessions. Rather, effective leaders motivate through inspiration, by encouraging their subordinates to motivate *themselves* in order to achieve success. Inspirational motivation, one of the five components of the transformational leadership theory, refers to leaders who inspire and motivate followers to reach ambitious goals previously deemed unreachable, thereby raising expectations, and communicating confidence that followers can achieve ambitious goals (a modified Pygmalion effect).

In his article "Motivation Employees Is Not Rocket Science", noted speaker and author Tim Connor offered an interesting perspective:

First of all it's not your job to motivate them. The concept of motivation implies that it is the responsibility of people to motivate themselves. As long as you see it as your responsibility to motivate them, guess what, you will always have to motivate them by finding clever, creative and innovative ways to accomplish this and trust me sooner or later you will tire of this responsibility. It is better to have them understand that their motivation is their responsibility not yours as their manager. Motivation is an inside-out not an outside in individual responsibility. The role of a manager is only to create a positive motivating, validating and empowering motivational climate in which employees are willing to take full responsibility for their own motivation.

Connor goes on to write that you can't bribe followers with cash, trinkets, and other incentives. In fact, many research studies have concluded that money doesn't rank near the top of the lists of things that motivate employees to perform. The best motivation in the world is to empower everyone within the organization to be the best that they can be. You can't force them, trick them, or threaten them. All you can do is inspire them. And the best way to inspire them is to lead by example.

Chapter 9: Learner

Effective leaders are perpetual learners. They can analyze successes and failures and learn from both experiences. I once read an anonymous quote that resonated with me: *"To live, learn; to learn, live. The deepest and most lasting joys of life spring from knowing and understanding the world about you and lessons may be had from every experience."* If you have children, you know how important it is to allow your children to learn from their mistakes. Sometimes it's a painful lesson, but a lesson nonetheless. I have been fortunate enough in my life to learn from every success and failure that I've experienced. If I hadn't flunked out of college early in life, I would've never learned the importance of dedication and perseverance. Those lessons propelled me to return to college later in life, even inspiring me to eventually earn my doctorate.

My life has taught me lessons at every turn, and I echo Tim Connor's sentiments regarding living and learning:

The opportunity for personal growth or learning can be found in each of life's experiences or teachers. The key to success is to learn to bring all of the learning back to yourself and not to point your finger or blame others or life for your teachers. You and I don't get to choose the curriculum in our lives or the lives of others, and we certainly don't get to choose how other people should learn their lessons. Everyone is on their unique path through life into their future.

Many years ago, I met with a customer who relayed an interesting story about the power of a lesson learned:

I recently empowered my shipping division to come up with a way to streamline the delivery process for our products. I really wanted them to think "out of the box", so I offered a cash bonus for the person who submitted the best idea, and promised to implement it. Well, we got the idea, implemented it, and it was a disaster. The delivery process actually got worse before we stepped in to re-evaluate what to do. After cleaning up the mess, I still paid the cash bonus to the employee. He took a chance that didn't work, and it wasn't his fault. I wanted him to remember that even though he didn't succeed in this venture, he still learned something about himself, and we learned something about ourselves as well.

That leader was secure enough in his tenure to pay someone for a *bad idea*. He knew that this employee would never forget the lesson he learned from this experience. This example underscores the importance of effective leaders in 21st century organizations establishing learning cultures within their enterprises. Learning organizations are more adaptable in recognizing the skills needs of their stakeholders, and they provide opportunities to create learning events (acquiring new skills, remediating gaps in knowledge, conveying information and knowledge internally and externally, and more).

We can't always choose our learning experiences in life. Most of them happen when we least expect it. The important thing to remember is that these lessons are taught for a reason; they help you to become the leader you were destined to be. In their book *The Strategy Process: Concepts, Context, Cases*, Henry Mintzberg, Joseph Lampel, James Quinn, and Sumantra Ghoshal asserted that learning organizations are inhabited with leaders who engage in systems thinking. These leaders possess the ability to see the big picture and focus more on underlying trends and forces of change as opposed to just day-to-day events (which sounds suspiciously like strategic and visionary leadership traits).

Final Thoughts: Where do you go from here?

My hope in sharing the information in this book is that you gain some insight about the core traits that many effective leaders share. This short and concise content wasn't intended to be 400 pages worth of scientific comparison of the leadership styles of the 21st century. You're welcome to read my doctoral dissertation if you're interested in a more scholarly examination of leadership effectiveness. Instead, this book was simply an opportunity for me to offer you a closer look at what makes effective people operate so...effectively.

I commend you on your decision to answer the call of leadership. If it were easy, everyone would do it. But because it's so difficult to lead others, your commitment is even more commendable. You have proven that something inside of you is superior to the challenges and opposition that you face as a leader. To every effective leader, don't rest on your laurels. You still have hills to climb and miles to go before you can rest. You should applaud yourself for your accomplishments, but don't overlook the challenges that lie ahead.

To every aspiring leader, be prepared to dig in and be the very best leader that you can be. Don't just be satisfied with your title or position – commit yourself to leaving a lasting legacy of effective leadership in your organization. The true test of your tenure is what happens when you're no longer there. I'll leave you with the words of author and speaker Jim Clemmer: *"Effective leaders generate action. Leadership is action, not a position."*

About the Author

Dr. Tony Bolden is the Principal and Chief Evangelist of Tony Bolden Enterprises, an advisory firm focused on leadership development and personal branding. With 30 years of experience in talent management, Tony is a Speaker, Author, Trainer, Facilitator, Advisor, and Organizational Behaviorist.

Some of his clients have included The Technology Association of Georgia – Human Resources Council; The Loss Prevention Foundation; The American Society of Association Executives; The National Business Travelers Association; The National Conference of Student Services; Future Business Leaders of America/Phi Beta Lambda, Inc.; Junior Achievement of America; The National Black Law Students Association; Phi Beta Sigma Fraternity, Inc.

Tony earned an MBA in Organizational Psychology & Development, and a Doctor of Management in Organizational Leadership, with a research focus of sales leadership and development. He and his family reside in suburban Atlanta, GA.

The 9 Signs of Effective Leadership Quiz

THE 9 SIGNS OF EFFECTIVE LEADERSHIP

Here are the descriptions of the nine core traits of effective leadership. This isn't a psychological assessment and there are no trick questions...so don't study too hard. This quiz is not meant to embarrass you; it's merely a "roadmap" to assist you in your quest to become an effective leader. Give yourself a score of 1-10 for each trait:

1. *Flexibility* – Able to adapt to dynamic environments with ease and speed. Thrives on change.

2. *Low Aversion to Risk* – Able to take and manage <u>appropriate</u> risks and use them to the organization's advantage. Can venture into the unknown and allow others to take steps to outpace the "competition".

3. *Knowledgeable* – Knowledgeable about trends, practices and policies affecting the industry and the organization. Has a good grasp of effective strategies and tactics that will positively impact the organization.

4. **Visionary** – Creates and communicates an inspired sense of purpose. Leads with a vision of the future, not the reality of today. Solicits opportunities and communicates effectively with others.

5. **Change Resilient** – Can cope with and embrace change, and use it to your advantage. Able to act without having the "total picture".

6. **Strategic** – Can see ahead clearly and anticipate consequences and trends accurately. Has broad knowledge and perspective; articulates vision, possibilities, strategies and plans.

7. **Communicator** – Relates well to diverse stakeholders inside and outside the organization. Able to influence and stimulate others, and build constructive relationships.

8. **Motivator** – Able to inspire, motivate and persuade others, communicates and "sells" the vision of the future.

9. **Learner** – A quick learner. Can analyze successes and failures and learn from both experiences.

Score Chart:

75 – 90

You're probably already in the Leadership role, and if not, you will be soon! You exhibit most or all of the qualities required to be an effective Leader!

60 – 75

You're off to a great start. You may need to work on the competencies that you scored low on, but you are an aspiring Leader.

59 or less

You have some of the basics, but you still have some growing to do. Stay committed, work on your low-scoring competencies and KEEP MOVING!

Referenced Resources

Knowledge Management: Challenges, Solutions, and Technologies – Irma Becerra-Fernandez, Avelino Gonzalez, and Rajiv Sabherwal

The Challenges of Leadership in the Modern World – Warren Bennis

Virtuoso Teams: Lessons From Teams That Changed Their Worlds – Andy Boynton and Bill Fisher

An Integrative Theory of Leadership – Martin Chemers

Pathways to Performance – Jim Clemmer

"Motivation Employees Is Not Rocket Science" – Tim Connor

"Who Me, Change?" – Peter de Jager

The Path of Least Resistance – Robert Fritz

The Organization of the Future – Doug Miller

The Strategy Process: Concepts, Context, Cases – Henry Mintzberg, Joseph Lampel, James Quinn, and Sumantra Ghoshal

Team Players and Teamwork: New Strategies for Developing Successful Collaboration – Glenn Parker

Right Risk – Bill Treasurer

Knowledge Emergence: Social, technical, and evolutionary dimensions of knowledge creation – Ikujiro Nonaka and Toshihiro Nishiguchi

The 9 Signs "Take Action!" Workbook

FLEXIBILITY

You're able to adapt to dynamic environments with ease and speed.

Leaders are often thrust into challenging environments and called upon to develop solutions – quickly. People find it difficult to follow a rigid leader. If you can't react to the ebb and flow of life, then you'll frustrate everyone around you. Effective leaders are like soldiers on the battlefield; they learn to adapt to any circumstance the find themselves in.

There are three enemies to flexibility:

1. <u>Tradition</u>

2. <u>Insecurity</u>

3. <u>Procrastination</u>

TAKE ACTION!

List three things you can do **today** to become a more *flexible* leader:

1.

2.

3.

THE BOTTOM LINE

"Man is an animal who more than any other can adapt himself to all climates and circumstances." **Henry David Thoreau**

Low Aversion to Risk

You're able to take and manage appropriate risks and use them to your advantage.

Let's face it: we don't like to venture beyond our comfort zone. Unfortunately, we live in a society where people desire more but want to sacrifice less to get it. You have to move beyond your comfort zone to get what you want. All progress involves risk. Sometimes it's measured risk, sometimes it "cliff jumping, death defying" risk – but its risk nonetheless. Effective leaders must learn how to take appropriate risks in order to advance their organizations. In order to take appropriate risks, you must:

1. Weigh your options

2. Consider the consequences

3. Use wise judgment

TAKE ACTION!

List three things you can do **today** to *lower your aversion to risk* and enhance your leadership:

1.

2.

3.

THE BOTTOM LINE

"Progress always involves risk; you can't steal second base and keep your foot on first." **Frederick Wilcox**

Knowledgeable

You're knowledgeable about trends, practices, and policies affecting the organization.

Every effective leader will tell you that they have a voracious desire to learn – no one wants to be on the outside of the information bubble. Knowledge is power. The more knowledge you have, the better prepared you are to lead your organization. One of the worst mistakes you can make as a leader is to make a decision without gathering all available information.

In order to lead effectively, you must have knowledge of:

1. Past practices, policies, & trends that have affected the organization

2. Current practices, policies, & trends that are affecting the organization

TAKE ACTION!

List three things you can do **today** to increase your *knowledge* and enhance your leadership:

1.

2.

3.

THE BOTTOM LINE

"The more extensive a man's knowledge of what has been done, the greater will be his power of knowing what to do". **Benjamin Disraeli**

Visionary

You create and communicate an inspired sense of purpose.

You lead with a vision of the future, not just the reality of today.

Webster's dictionary defines a visionary is someone who *"envisions things in perfect but unrealistic form; idealistic"*. I take exception to the term *"unrealistic"* because I fervently believe that if you want to effectively lead you must lead with a vision of the future and not just the reality of today. An effective leader must look beyond things as they are now and see them for what they *could* be. Being a true visionary means:

1. Seeing the "big picture"
2. Treating your challenges like opportunities.

TAKE ACTION!

List three things you can do **today** to hone your *vision* for your organization and enhance your leadership:

1.

2.

3.

THE BOTTOM LINE

"Vision without action is merely a dream. Action without vision just passes the time. Vision with action can change the world". **Joel Barker**

Change Resilient

You can cope with and embrace change, and use it to your advantage.

For most of us, it's difficult to embrace change because of the uncertainty that's involved. Some of us spend our lives trying to avoid change. Fear of change results in sacrificing growth for the sake of stability. Effective leaders don't worry about what happened – instead, they focus on what needs to happen next. Effective leaders understand that:

1. Change is inevitable

2. There is no real safety in your "comfort zone"

TAKE ACTION!

List three things you can do **today** to embrace the concept of *change* and enhance your leadership:

1.

2.

3.

THE BOTTOM LINE

"Change can be exhilarating, joyous, liberating. But it can also be terrifying, because, in a deeper sense, you are questioning your very identity and sense of value.
But take the risk. It's worth it." **Dee Hock**

Strategic

You can see clearly ahead and anticipate consequences

& trends accurately.

Effective leaders are very strategic when it comes to charting the course for their organizations. Sometimes you must act quickly and make decisions based on your knowledge and instinct, but you shouldn't always be in "reactive" mode. You can ensure a semblance of balance by developing a strategic plan, and sticking to the plan you develop. What does a strategic plan really look like? Quite simply, a strategic plan is a written plan that details:

1. <u>Where you are now</u>
2. <u>Where you want to be</u>
3. <u>The internal and external factors that can help and hinder you</u>
4. <u>How you will know when you "get there"</u>

TAKE ACTION!

List three things you can do **today** to become more *strategic* and enhance your leadership:

1.

2.

3.

THE BOTTOM LINE

"To map out a course of action and follow it to an end requires...courage." **Ralph Waldo Emerson**

Communicator

You relate well to diverse stakeholders inside and outside of the organization. You're able to influence and stimulate others, and build constructive relationships.

It's useless to be a creative, innovative leader if you can't successfully communicate your vision to those around you. As the leader, it's your job to "see the vision" and be able to articulate it to others. To be an effective communicator within your organization, you must be accessible. You have to avail yourself and listen to the thoughts, ideas, and concerns of those around you. You'll never be "in touch" with those around you if your voice is the only one that's heard. How can enhance communication within your organization?

1. <u>Solicit ideas and feedback from those around you</u>

2. <u>Watch what you do in addition to what you say!</u>

TAKE ACTION!

List three things you can do **today** to become a more effective *communicator* and enhance your leadership brand:

1.

2.

3.

THE BOTTOM LINE

"What you say is only the beginning. Your behavior, your actions, and your decisions are also ways of communicating, and leaders have to learn how to create a consistent message through all of these."
David Thomas

Motivator

You're able to inspire, motivate and persuade others.

You have to inspire those around you to reach for greatness if you want your organization to enjoy sustained success. Your followers should be as excited about the future as you are. As leaders, we need to engage the hearts and minds of those who toil with us day in and day out. Motivating others can be a very tricky proposition. You don't want to bribe them, but you don't want to intimidate them either. There are 2 traditional methods for motivating others:

1. Fear or Punishment (Based on threat of withdrawal of a privilege).

2. Reward or Incentive (Based on the wants or needs)

The only way to truly motivate others is to empower them to motivate themselves. You can't force or trick them – all you can do is lead by example and inspire.

TAKE ACTION!

List three things you can do **today** to *motivate* those around you and enhance your leadership:

1.

2.

3.

THE BOTTOM LINE

"In motivating people, you've got to engage their minds and their hearts."

Learner

You can analyze successes and failures and learn

from previous experiences.

You will never grow as an effective leader if you can't learn from the positive and negative experiences in your life. Ideally, we'd like to learn in the most comfortable situations. The truth, however, is that we learn the most from some of our devastating and catastrophic failures. The true tragedy of any failure is to not recognize the learning opportunity, thus increasing the propensity to repeat the failure in the future. Abraham Lincoln said *"my great concern is not whether you fail, but rather that you are content with your failure"*. The best way to learn from success is to evaluate what went *right*. The best way to learn from failure is to evaluate what went *wrong*.

TAKE ACTION!

List three things you can do **today** to become a more effective *learner* and enhance your leadership:

1.

2.

3.

THE BOTTOM LINE

"To live, learn; to learn, live. The deepest and most lasting joys of life spring from knowing and understanding the world about you and lessons may be had from every experience." **Source Unknown**

CALL TO ACTION:

Consider the key points you read in this book and document the "take-aways" you consider to be the most valuable...

_____

_____

_____

_____

_____

_____

_____

_____

_____

_____

_____

_____

_____

_____

_____

_____

_____

_____

_____

_____

_____

_____

_____

CALL TO ACTION:

What are 3 things you can do within the first month after reading this book to begin implementing the "take-aways" you identified?

_____

_____

_____

_____

_____

_____

_____

_____

_____

_____

_____

_____

_____

_____

_____

_____

_____

_____

_____

_____

_____

_____

_____

_____

_____

_____

_____

_____

_____

_____

_____

_____

_____

_____

_____

_____

_____

_____

_____

_____

_____

_____

_____

_____

_____

_____

_____

_____

_____

_____

_____

Made in the USA
Monee, IL
31 January 2024

52323692R00049